I0756254

FINISHING LINE PRESS
www.finishinglinepress.com

My Mother's Hands

meditations from the Finger Lakes

poems by

Cory Brown

Finishing Line Press
Georgetown, Kentucky

My Mother's Hands

meditations from the Finger Lakes

ISBN 979-8-89990-467-7 First Edition

ACKNOWLEDGMENTS

Cloudbank: "Understanding Russian," "Confrontation," and "But Here's the Thing"
The Comstock Review: "Something Strange" and "Quandary" (Special Recognition, Muriel Bailey competition)
december: "Friday the 13th"
LitMag: "Giant Sequoias" (Runner-up, Anton Chekhov flash fiction competition)
Mudfish: "Boomerang," "Reality," and "My Mother's Hands" (as "What We Know")
Nimrod International Literary Journal: "To Live" and "What I'd Thought"
Oberon Poetry: "Out in the Deep" (Honorable Mention, Oberon poetry competition)

I thank writer Nancy Menning and musicologist Sara Haefeli for reading and editing drafts of this collection as well as those of my three previous books, and my wife, Xanthe Matychak, for her love and support.

Publisher: Leah Huete de Maines
Editor: Christen Kincaid
Cover Art: Fernando Llosa
Author Photo: Xanthe Matychak
Cover Design: Elizabeth Maines McCleavy

Order online: www.finishinglinepress.com
also available on amazon.com

Author inquiries and mail orders:
Finishing Line Press
PO Box 1626
Georgetown, Kentucky 40324
USA

Contents

Understanding Russian

Woke up one morning recently realizing that for the previous few days I'd been grieving my own death. I think it's a good feeling, generally, when you realize what you've only been intuiting. It constitutes, maybe, a release, presumably from a burden, but what's the burden? Perhaps feeling that something's going on that you're not aware of and whatever it is matters to you. Finding out about it is like being in a crowded elevator with people who are talking about you without knowing you're there, so you're hearing the truth. It doesn't matter if it's bad, it's the truth. Finally—and you feel it—you're on the same page as the rest of the universe. This happens in the film version of *The Queen's Gambit*, when the Russian champion and our heroine are in an elevator at the hotel where a tournament is being held. The two are about to play one another and the Russian begins explaining to his assistant standing next to him, in Russian, our heroine's defects as a player, how she gets angry in the middle of games and loses her composure, "like a typical woman," he adds. The Russian, on the other hand, our heroine discovers upon playing him that day, comports himself throughout every game with absolute equanimity, like a machine, she later describes him—every move calculated and "precise." I sometimes wish I could've moved through my life like the Russian plays chess, not dispassionate exactly, just calm and knowing. *Wisely* might be the right word. I wish I'd behaved more wisely. So the elevator is crowded and the Russian and his assistant don't see her in the back and even if they did probably wouldn't suspect that being American, from Kentucky, she knows Russian and can understand what they're saying. This morning after my coffee, I took the dog outside and emptied the compost at the back of the yard. It was muggy and hot, but there was a slight breeze that made me say to myself "I love summer," and the garlic was mostly green still, not burnt to make them look like the stalks of ripe wheat they'll look like in a few days, the blackcap raspberries ripening, skies clear, a few clouds gathering in the west, and I'd heard there was a thunderstorm coming this afternoon to save us from a prolonged dry spell. That was a moment when I was in a crowded elevator and the universe was talking about me in Russian, saying I was going to die, and I understood every word.

Port Jefferson Beach

Psychologists call knowing your life's meaning "presence." People low in presence don't bother searching—they're "stuck." Those high in presence but still searching are called "seekers." —Arthur Brooks, "The Meaning of Life is Surprisingly Simple," The Atlantic

Brooks writes that some people, Albert Camus was one, believe there isn't any meaning to life and that that makes everything possible. My wife and I walked along the beach yesterday here in Port Jefferson where she grew up. She wanted to relive the feeling of a morning on this beach, which is very rocky. I couldn't help but marvel at how much variety there was among the rocks—sizes, shapes, colors—no two alike. It was a beautiful morning and all the rocks a few feet from the water were wet even though the tide was coming in, not going out. A mystery to me, but my wife was unpuzzled by it. She has more presence than I, I'm sure, whereas I'm still searching, or stuck, not sure which, which may mean the whole project is hopeless for me. I wondered why, for example, rocks when wet take on a different look—they glow. It's as if they come alive. My wife picked up a couple and skipped them across the still surface of the bay. A clue in today's crossword puzzle, it just so happens, was "alternative to rocks," and the answer it turned out was "neat." You may think it's asking about rocks when it's referencing cocktails. But isn't that what happens so often? You'll be humming along thinking everything you're thinking and the context changes. You're on a car trip worrying about gas and your tire blows, your child in the back seat starts choking, or your spouse starts talking about some plan she has for you next year that you hadn't expected. Now, are you lucky if the context you live in is forever the same? Maybe not, maybe it makes you think the context is the same for everyone, or should be, which is worse, thinking you know what's best for all. You might live in one little town your whole life, for example, and expect that town to be the steady-as-she-goes life for you and everyone you know. But that doesn't keep your friends alive, you healthy, or your spouse, if you have one, loving and faithful. Shit happens in small towns, too, we all know that. I remember when I was young watching my father break down crying after hearing that our long-time dentist, who lived in a small town near us where my father's mother lived, shot himself in the heart with a shotgun. That was a shock to my father, though I would not have thought so given he'd been in combat in Italy, wounded twice. But this was a different context: many years after the war, small town back in the states, peacetime, and, most different, suicide. I doubt he saw many suicides in combat. So even experience doesn't always prepare us for shifts in context. Camus wrote that suicide is the only philosophical issue worthy of our attention. Interesting idea, but it might not be my issue, or yours. Maybe yours is cancer, or emphysema, which recently took one of my oldest and dearest friends because, probably, he'd smoked most of his life. He loved life so was likely in no danger of killing himself. Camus, it turns out, ain't no Solomon, after all.

Boomerang

It is not a boomerang but a bundle of bailing wire my brother has arranged
and it's how we send our love to one another sometimes in the field
when you're a good ways away and need some wire about the length and
weight of a boomerang though not a boomerang in that it's not to come
back at all that my brother sends flying at my father standing while busy
with something on the trailer with his head down busy with something
as I watch it in the air like a boomerang spinning and coming toward
his face and there we are at one of his auctions the farmers all standing
around under the tent or sitting on bales and waiting for my father the
auctioneer to begin or saying their goodbyes to their neighbors my brother
standing near them but away from me and my father and tossing to us
that much needed wire and I'm tired bored and depressed I'm sure from
some heartache teenager that I am but this is a long time ago a memory I
don't know how accurate except that boomerang flying at my father's face
I'm standing there not knowing if I hate this man or not with his military
silencing act that may not be as much of an act as I think it is but more
my being the youngest of five not knowing how to sit with chastisement
and shame while he's had his fill of children after all these years maybe
and through the air comes that boomerang at the auction about to start or
maybe finishing up with the farmers all bunched up like a bundle of wire a
congregation of churchgoers watching and hearing about the suffering all
those many years ago and considering the width and depth of their own
sins and it's hot as hell this being western Oklahoma and all and a summer
memory as I said so maybe a nice spring day or maybe 110 I can't lay claim
to any certainty other than that bundle of wire flying toward my father's
face that I remember clear as day as they say though not that many things
in this sublunar world are with his head down attending to something in his
grave now over twenty-five years and my brother as well almost three now
standing there incredulous that I'm the paralytic that I am in that moment
that afternoon that morning month season of the year that bundle of wire
like a boomerang but not a boomerang closing in on my father's face

Upon Hearing My Mother Cry in the Night

I couldn't believe what I was hearing in that house small enough for
seven people to hear whatever was said from any of the seven mouths
and whatever could she possibly be crying about there in bed late at night
with the darkness all around us and our well-oiled family all seven of us
running around like a new car or pickup right off the lot as smoothly as I
could imagine a family could run with cattle to water and feed and fences
to mend and gardens to tend, but then I heard her say through the tears,
Why can't they aim better? and I knew then it was the pee on the toilet seat
in our bathroom in the very corner of the house a room just big enough
to stand in but there it was with its pee-stained toilet that when cleaning it
must've stared back at her—the toilet water mirroring her life years later as
a widow without my father to listen to her crying in the dark and even later
too though this time like a ghost of herself her own body six feet under that
is what I think now she likely saw that night in the toilet and I ask myself
now why we three did not take it upon ourselves but then oh then it was a
doll-house we lived in and a prince mustn't think about such lowly duties
prancing around aiming his pee wherever he pleased though perhaps not
altogether where she would've chosen him to aim not the landing spot of
her choosing I suspect and nor surely was such a thing on her mind when
she agreed to marry this man from Oklahoma whisking her away from
the snow-crusted soil and ice-crusted large lakes and hills and valleys of
northern Vermont full of snow and more snow and pee-stained toilets were
not I would guess what she had in mind when he proposed with his pretty
wavy red hair and chest full of medals for fending off those wicked Nazis
across the pond that handsome hero who'd flirted with her on the steps of
the Capitol Building in 1942 before all those lovely letters came back to her
from the violent war-torn Apennines with their quiet promise between each
and every line of a spotless happiness

Return of the Cicadas

...I want the old July, but old July was awful,
green bugs and strangers. I want the new July,
the sidewalk of it, the noise of dispute or affection
on loan....
Mike Loughran, "One Two Three"

All this talk of old and new and waking up again makes me happy that the old will be restored, after all. Cicadas will come back and not just to haunt us, but to sing to us. Yes, the old July was awful, but it's still breathing, as all history is, like a guppy in a fishbowl. Aren't we all on our own gasping for air in a fishbowl clouded with algae while outside cicada shells cling to tree bark like damsels in distress. As for you, your fingers and feet are fine, your kidneys Harley Davidsons humming down the road on a warm summer evening and if you want, you can give it all away. Give what away, you ask? Why, everything of course. The sun will shine on your bare feet even if your big brother has passed, the one who used to fight on the living-room carpet with your other big brother, big-horned goats clashing, and all you could do with their anger was curl up in the corner like a poisoned bug. Just remember to remove your shoes; otherwise, they'll cast dark shadows with every step and those shadows will portend bad things for your grandchildren, the ones who will have forgotten both you and the difference between past and future perfect. And they will suffer both common and exotic diseases and work their whole lives to pay the piper for their musical cures. So remove your shoes: earthing, the young ones call it, the ones who vape and suspect it may not be good for them, but they like the participle part of it, which makes them think things are moving up for them nice and easy like smoke. They suppose it's better than a quart of gin a day, but blind ignorance can presuppose a dangerous freedom and about that gin: I would do it if I could but I'm afraid it would give me bad dreams, of cavernous halls filled with importunate voices and I am wandering around not knowing how to escape what seems like a party or a high school reunion. Or is it a wake? That's when you know it's time to acknowledge the azaleas blooming outside your bedroom window and next to them the mock orange blossoms making their lovely way into your future, yours and that of all the bugs and bacteria working in the earth, like little Roman gladiators, to assure the soil and all creatures great and small of their eminent viability.

The Cloud of Unknowing

The introduction tells me of the 14th century debate among theologians East & West regarding the more apt descriptor of our understanding of god, positive or negative. The East preferred positive, with terms like love, light, life, might, etc. The West does not, as one might expect, prefer the opposing terms to describe what god repudiates, such as hate, darkness, and squalor. No, they argued that whatever words or concepts we use are meaningless because we don't have the capacity for it (except, we might say, for gendering). We are finite, he is eternal. It's as if we have a sort of anosmia of understanding. Just as those with that condition can't smell or taste, we can't experience his qualities by way of the intellect. The ambiguity is referred to as *the cloud of unknowing*. He's not unknowable though, the author says, just indescribable. He is indeed approachable by way of love. The paradox here is not so much that this is an argument for the ineptness of argument, but that this practice is said to function positively. When you focus in your prayers not on god's attributes, nor on your own sinfulness, but on "the shadow of his love," not only can you begin to approach his sublimity, but you are obviating a need for repentance. And because you are saturated by his love, thoughts that might otherwise lead you down the primrose path of dalliance simply don't arise. This you, the text argues, what we'd call ego, disappears in the cloud to become one with it. A decent approach to the mystery of existence, if you ask me, even secular, giving oneself over to the mystery without a preordained sense of self.

The anosmia analogy came to mind I'm sure because I've had it now myself—the physical variety—for four months, most likely from covid, though I tested negative twice when sick back in June. Whatever the virus, it's lasted longer than a few days. I can identify classes of food. A bite of toast with strawberry jam I can sense is sweet. What becomes important in the weak pleasures of this condition are other aspects, textures and their contrasts, for example—the crispness of fried halibut's batter and the softness of the flesh within. It's a curious condition, providing in my mind intimations of mortality, one of several recently: I recall years ago my 85-year-old grandmother, her swollen ankles propped up on an ottoman, side-by-side paintings of Jesus and JFK hanging above her head, saying she's ready to die, she can't taste anything anymore; this morning my doctor said my numbers still indicate diabetes; my dermatologist just called to say the biopsy on the cutting she took yesterday is positive for squamous cell carcinoma; a high school friend texted me last week to say that a friend of ours who'd been in hospice has died, breast cancer.

I'm in the backyard sipping coffee, savoring its warmth, and from my chair I think I saw a few minutes ago high in the trees a Red-headed Piliated Woodpecker. I took a picture of it on my phone, then heard it making its call, which I swear could be mistaken for a monkey's. When I looked for it in the photograph, though, its splendor in the leafy heavens, there was no hint of it. It's late September now and those leaves will begin to fall soon. I looked again, zooming in this time. Nada. I think I love that woodpecker.

Giant Sequoias

I didn't belong there—that was my first feeling. Years ago, the Grand Canyon had made me feel this way, but here I felt more closed in, unsurprisingly, the sensation more intense, the air hushed as if we were about to hear Amazing Grace or a Shakespeare sonnet: "To me, fair friend, you never can be old, / For as you were when first your eye I ey'd / Such seems your beauty still." Such seems their beauty still, though fat chance we'd have seen them young, the elders as saplings about 1000 B.C.E., before the Roman Empire, the Han and Tang dynasties, Alexander the Great, Epicurus, Atilla the Hun, Confucius, Gautama, Nebuchadnezzar, Sappho. Before all the great Greek dramatists these beauties were soaking up sunshine and spring melts and there I was among them just last week. With my brother, his son, and a friend, we'd hiked Hetch Hetchy for three days, but the heat drove us back to the car and we decided to pay homage to these mammoths of the Sierra Nevadas. I approached the base of one and stepped off fifteen feet around half of it, then felt foolish, as if a few steps could take the measure of such a thing. We're told they're as old and big as they are because they grow fast and their climate nurtures them: a mile or so up so it's not too hot, lots of water from melting snowpacks, and few damaging fires—until now, that is. The biggest here stretches up almost 300 feet, named General Sherman, which is ironic because Sherman was known for his destructive burning, and though they need fire to release seeds from their cones they're now going up in smoke at a disturbing rate, a fifth of them just last year. Their bark is said to protect them from flames, but some are burnt black and hang off them like ratty old overcoats. Still, they look majestic and wise, these giants, as if they harbored thousands of stories, having witnessed generations warring one after another, unrecovered warriors rotting at their feet, young lovers risking everything to meet under their limbs at night, new religions shaped in their afternoon shade. Before Europeans, the Western Monos were there, who speak a Uto-Aztecan language, and many still are, northwest of there near Madira, and in the Eastern section of the park were the Shoshonean-speaking Tubatulabal, some now living in the Kern River Valley south of there. They have their religions, of course, but it seems these trees could be their own religion, the path through the grove wide and quiet like an aisle in a grand cathedral, the contrast between us insects and their enormity overwhelming. God, it seemed, was in them…or is them. Ah, how crafty of her, I thought. Don't look *in* me, their size and grandeur insisted, look at me, for I am the thing itself! I felt them in my bones—the pieces of them, the broken off limbs from centuries past scattered as if the mountainside was their own cemetery. Not ghoulish, though, since they don't rot, we're told because of tannin in their bark and heartwood. One of them farther up the path was felled over a hundred years ago, the sign said, then hollowed out so visitors could walk through, a tunnel through its corpse. I walked in and observed a sacrilege of old carvings, Clara + Franky, Bonnie + Howard, folks maybe long dead, I thought, and where o where are their great loves now? There in the belly I began to feel the pangs of all lost loves, romantic and otherwise, Jonah with seaweed around his head and all the sailors buried in the deep having never been vomited onto dry land. I thought of poor deluded Ahab with his dark sufferings, Queequeg and his heroics all for naught, of Ophelia, Cordelia, and Anna Karenina and their tragic lives, Joe Christmas and his, and all the forgotten dead in reality: ninety percent of American Indigenous by the end of the 19th century killed by guns and European diseases; I thought of all those across the world burnt alive or drawn and quartered for religious transgressions; all those murdered by racists and ideologues, the thousands of Polish and Ukrainian fathers, mothers, sons, daughters, infants, as early as 1938 shot in the head with pistols or gunned down with rifles by ordinary middle-aged Germans conscripted for the killings, the *SS Einsatzgruppen*, before and during the gassings at Chelmno, Treblinka, Auschwitz-Birkenau, Sobibor, and elsewhere across Europe; the WWI soldiers obliterated by bombs, shot down, gassed, at Verdun, Ypres, Gallipoli, the Somme, the Argonne Forest; all the Hindus and Muslims caught on the wrong side of the border in 1948; immigrants lost, drowned, starved, beaten to death for wanting to live somewhere safe; two-hundred years of conquistadors shooting, burning, hacking Mayans to death; Roman vestal virgins executed by immurement for breaking their vows; the millions of abducted Africans in cargo holds starved, beaten, murdered, drowned; thousands of prisoners in U. S. Civil War camps starved to death or killed by diseases at Andersonville, Camp Douglas, Elmira; prisoners of war everywhere brutalized, hung, shot by firing squads; soldiers across the world accused of cowardice and shot or hung; unsuspecting civilians incinerated at Dresden, Hamburg, London, Tokyo, Hiroshima, Nagasaki; millions of women across the world raped by soldiers; millions of women across the world dead from pregnancy or childbirth, from complications, preeclampsia, high blood pressure; children everywhere born dead or killed at the hands of "protectors," by disease or hunger, left on the streets to starve and die, forgotten or sold into slavery, prostitution. And the sufferings from more natural disasters: those buried in avalanches of mud, snow, rock; those woken in the night by smoke in their own houses, their own beds, suffocating before the flames engulfed them; those caught in the woods or desert, collapsed from exhaustion and thirst; those with their body parts scattered at plane crash sites; those whose bodies were crushed in their own cars; those who thought their cars would've shielded them from rushing waters; those trapped by hurricanes on their upper floors, drowned before anyone could reach them; those caught in their own trailer houses torn apart by tornadoes; those who suffocated and are suffocating today from respiratory viruses; all the uninsured cancer patients choosing death as a condition of having lived; terminally ill children whose parents can't believe a god would let their baby, their own child born from love, suffer pancreatic, lung, or liver cancer, leukemia, multiple myeloma, skin or brain cancer, a god who would let the dark cells multiply and migrate like spring flowers, like trillium or phlox. Back in the open air, it was Basho who came to mind, his trek through the northern country, the forests and the deep snows. He often wrote of crying in response to the beauty of a natural scene and I was always skeptical about it. Tears brought on by a temple whose priest had died, a friend he may've known from his younger days, I could understand, but a sliver moon? a quiet snowfall in the mountains? the Milky Way arched over a stormy sea? So when I felt it coming on, I thought, okay old poet, you win.

Friday the 13th

For some it's the intimacy they're afraid of, or the absence of it, or not knowing which it is, what they want, confused by what they're told they should want. This is the horror of horrors, blood dripping from the bunkbed above where lies a dead boy with blank eyes. In the same cabin the girl has just had sex with her boyfriend and is running into the rain in her underwear to go pee. The boyfriend in the lower bunk lights a post-coital cigarette and the blood drips onto his cheek, which signals his doom. Meanwhile, in the camp's bathroom the girl is about to step in her own pee, so to speak, an ax about to land in her forehead. The movie implies she deserves it because she went out in the rain in just her panties and no one does that. But showing us some skin gives us a glimpse of our own desires, the peek-a-boo Hitchcock said was the source of all his fears, his mother playing that game with him when he was three. And just like that we see that the real horror is our own doing, voices we recognize as our own, thoughts ours and ours alone, dreams only we could dream, the ones we walk out of when we wake up in the morning, shaping our days into little balls, our spidery legs spinning and spinning. But what do you really want? someone asked me just before I woke.

But Here's the Thing

I sometimes want to dumpster dive just to smell how bad things can get. I think pain could be my friend, if I let it. If I let it deflect the other. The other pain. The one that is unnamable. *Deflect* is what doctors call one pain replacing another, like those who have to cut themselves to keep from feeling the pain in their hearts. Or maybe it's *referred* pain I'm thinking of. Pain you feel in one part of your body caused by an injury to another. It's like when you go for a job interview because someone has referred you to them and maybe they like you for that but maybe they don't. Maybe they've already chosen someone but have to interview you to appease the person who referred you to them, so you're just taking up time in their day, the man with the round head and small eyes sipping on his fifth cup. He has to interview you when he could be doing his crossword puzzle or playing footsies with Debbie in accounting. Who wants to be interviewed by someone who'd rather be playing footsies with Debbie in accounting? And you can bet all the dead leaves falling off the trees come fall she doesn't even like him—thinks he's a creep. It's a slap in the face to both you and Debbie. *But the truth is*...I've always liked that phrase, but the truth is. Almost as much as *but here's the thing*. When I hear someone say *but here's the thing* it makes me think everything's going to be all right, because they know what that thing is, whatever it is.

Out in the Deep

One evening on my back porch, looking out over the tomatoes and pumpkins in my garden, late fall but warm, I remembered a dream from a few nights before in which I was treading water in a large lake, friends circling in a ski boat to pick me up, the sunset coming on with its salmon-colored rays shooting up from the horizon. There I was in that 50 to a 100-foot-deep lake when I felt a hand grip my ankle. These days voices in my sleep make me grind my teeth and most of my dreams are uneventful. I remember in my early 20s spending an afternoon in the country with a friend, lounging around a small pond. It must've been fall, for it was Oklahoma and not too cold or hot and the prairie grass around us was tall. I remember the wind and the smell of her hair when I leaned over to her, small ripples lapping against the pond's shore. I didn't think to just kiss her, and the other night when I woke to strange voices and music from outside or from nearby neighbors, I turned on the radio to drown it out and remembered the smell of her hair. We went into the water that afternoon, stripped down like Adam and Eve, like children who don't think anything of being naked with one another. She went under and grabbed my ankle just like in the dream and I went under too—the water thick with red silt—and I got close enough to see her hair and reach out for it, and I can remember feeling it floating in my fingers. We'd grown up in the same neighborhood, staying up late talking on her back porch until we were too tired to talk, and then a train would whistle a few blocks away and I'd imagine us walking to the track to press our palms against the warm steel that had soaked up the whole day's heat. I tried to see her once passing through the town she works in. I was about to leave the building when she appeared in her nurse's uniform like an angel or ghost, and later I imagined when she said goodbye in the cafeteria and kissed my cheek that she meant for the hint of perfume she left there to be a secret note slipped into my hand alluding to long lost allurements.

Sometimes Beauty is the Only Thing That Matters

In Wim Wenders' *Wings of Desire*, the angel Damiel has fallen in love with the melancholic trapeze artist Marion and by way of divine telepathy listens to her thoughts. In her despair she says to herself, "Sometimes beauty is the only thing that matters." His is a most beautiful face, the actor Bruno Ganz, and Marion's beauty is a given, the actress Solveig Donmartin, her character holding Damiel spellbound with her catatonic stares, and too in the ring as she twirls her risky acrobatics. Wenders captures the children's faces in black and white next to Damiel as they sit in the bleachers staring at Marion's twirling. I think the most beautiful thing I've seen are birds in flight, a seagull skimming inches above the surface of a glassy lake, or the Canadian geese I've been seeing these past few days migrating south, one phalanx morphing into another, Roman soldiers marching toward Visigoths, Visigoths toward Romans, these soldiers marching from cold fields and icy bodies of water to a warm climate with more grass and insects. The most striking example of birds in flight are the starlings that famously weave their shapes over Rome because, as researchers tell us, cities are warm and Rome's tropical temperatures accommodate their needs. We're told their pirouetting is how they decide where to land for the night, testing the air and gaining various views of the trees below. In one of Italo Calvino's novels the narrator, Mr. Palomar, observes from his terrace that the starlings shape themselves into circles resembling, Calvino writes, a cartoon speech-bubble above someone thinking of a sky full of birds—a visual onomatopoeia, the text mimicking what it denotes. I used to be in love with the beauty of language, letting words pirouette on the page, and though I'm no longer in thrall to it I can still admire its moments of charm. Montaigne's phrase "every metaphor limps" comes to mind. What a rich trope, a double-pirouette, a turn within a turn. I picture him sitting in his castle in the late afternoon, having witnessed that day an old man limping, twisting the image in his mind until it lands on the page like the autumn leaves today outside my window floating their way to the ground. Of all the arts, I think dance the most beautiful, its vulgar athleticism sublimated into easy movements, its beauty in its simplicity, creating tension in our minds as we find it difficult to believe what we're seeing yet pleased by it nonetheless, as we are by the starlings painting their liquid portraits over Rome.

What I'd Thought

We're forever and tragically fleshing out the bones of our youth, babes in our cribs scared to be alone. The passion before and during some passing afternoon—a curtain blowing in and out of the window—was the summer bloom before autumn sank its claws in deep, the falling leaves all around us in the forest, bright yellow oaks, deep blood-colored maples, a matted floor of pine needles under us, one hand reaching for another. We had to commit no matter who we'd promised ourselves to, no matter who we'd inconceivably forgotten. It was as if we'd been forgiven already, our names thrown into the sea and washed up onshore. And we'd stay only as long as our blood burned in the night. Those times have walked away from us. Would that we had let the passion go like a horse we believe in with no pedigree, no history to speak of, a race with nothing at stake. We'd choose to be who we are, wedding rings put away in a drawer by the window. Some feelings are too easy to forget, our fragility cutting us to the bone. It's as if we had watched ourselves bleeding and not known what had cut us up in the night. If we'd known, we'd not have let ourselves fall, letting the warm breeze blow the curtains in and out without reading them like tarot cards. It would take years to mend, the same moon over our heads again and again, looking down on us and all the empty stares. We're people with bodies and no heads who think we're honoring love, think we're love itself. Now there are no times to recover. Summer has warmed the open window for years, the earth forgotten long ago what we'd done, the world again as green as grass, flesh grown anew. They had been self-seductions. Who would believe we do what we do for a reason? Did we love them, after all? Even if we'd let our fingers be the mere fishhooks they are, tongues ordinary tongues, we might have wished still to be the fish thrown back into the sea, curtains blowing in the breeze, faces in the soft cradling palms of our lover's hands, days and nights we thought numberless, numbered after all.

Quandary

What is it to consider one's non-existence, to surrender the question itself? Time is the operative dimension, the enriching element in this quandary, the early frost that kills as well as the gravy that makes the meal, provides the flavor to make a life a life. So the today in which we exist must pay homage to the tomorrow in which we will not. When Andrei Bolkonsky, adjutant to the general, one of our heroes in *War and Peace*, paces back and forth the evening before the battle at Borodino, where he will be wounded and die of it, he considers this question: *what is it to me that tomorrow I will cease to be?* He knows he did not love his wife and child as he should've and is asking himself how he could possibly make amends the evening before his demise. *What is this trial I am conducting on myself this evening,* he asks, *when my life will have no meaning after tomorrow?* On his deathbed, though, with his beloved Natasha knitting by his side, he has a vision of death as an awakening. *We are created for happiness*, writes Tolstoy, *and life is infinite and incomprehensible.* How are we to conceive of a world, I ask, in which the question of being can no longer be posed? Death is the gray afternoon of a gray day; it is the sun that confers meaning, infuses everything with life—every leaf dead or alive, every gap between clouds, between branches separated from one another fifty, a hundred, five-hundred years ago, every cloud of breath from our mouths in the cold air of Alaska, Newfoundland, Moscow, Baffin Bay, every open pore sweating in a desert heat, every eyelash of every mammal, tiger and mouse alike, every reptile's tooth in Madagascar, the Syrian desert, every antenna of each and every dragonfly, every corpuscle on every mountainside, even in the darkness of sea beds, the sun infusing them all with life.

My Mother's Hands

It's as if we've been uprooted by words, orphaned, from the Greek *orphanos*, "bereaved." My mother was bereaved as a child, orphaned at five by her mother. It was tuberculosis, from the Latin *tuber*, an underground structure that bears eyes or buds from which new plants arise. She was betrayed by a word, unstructured. Then she became a mother herself, several times over, in fact, and as the story goes cried when she heard she was pregnant with me, her fifth. Tears of joy they were not, but to know she cried for herself and not for me is to see her as someone other than my mother, other than a word. Yet, seeing her body in the casket, all the family gathered around her, her hands gnarled—from Middle English *knob* or *wood knot*—made me feel orphaned. They were my mother's hands, after all.

Wait Until Dark

I think lying in my grave, if I miss anything it will be sunlight. Perhaps we'll all bathe in it by way of grass or tree branches or ocean plants or patches of algae or some such. If so, those who have gone before us are doing so now. I remember sitting in the theater with my mother, my first time, ten years old, popcorn smell in the air, lights dimming, previews coming on making me later wish I'd seen *that* movie instead of this one, *Wait Until Dark*, Audrey Hepburn's character blind and being stalked for a stash of drugs she unwittingly has in her possession. Somehow the stalker is killed, Hepburn capitalizing on her blindness in her dark apartment. It was frightening, the violence, the crescendos, my mother and I very much alive to one another. Then we stepped out of the theater and into the fall air. Why this movie? A random choice perhaps, wanting merely to escape the dreariness or exhaustion of an ordinary afternoon. I looked out my window this morning and realized it's October, past her late September birthday and time for a new birth, a new season. If she were buried near here, or in Vermont where she grew up, there would be leaves piling their stunning colors onto her grave—yellow-green, russet, blood red. As it is, she lies in the high plains among oaks and cedars, family nearby, prairie grass above her bleached by the sun.

Wind Advisory

in memoriam, Butch Brown 1950-2020

The house has been whistling and groaning all morning long. "Wind advisory," they call it. What's the advice? I wonder. I'm reading Marcus Aurelius. He's the wind and I the house. "If you feel vexed by the evils in the world," he writes, "think of all the souls no longer vexed." I think of them lying down now in their own place of worship, six feet under or at the bottom of the sea or some large or small body of water, like the little pond on campus a student of mine found himself in in the middle of the night a few years ago, a cold night. Intentional? We don't know. Or think about all those lost souls who made their interesting journey through some creature's bowels—we've been around, after all, a lot longer than we've been comfy in our overstuffed chairs sipping on tea, munching on crumpets. "Don't ever feel left out," Aurelius adds: "Rest assured you too will be absorbed into the whole, the fiery spirit of the universe from which we all come." Do they serve good coffee there, a slice of apple pie, whipped cream? The storm has quieted, though the chimes on the porch sway, ring out. A beeping in the house I can't tell from where—the timer in the kitchen? The bell tolls for thee, I hear it singing. Oh, it's my tea. I sip on it and read: "You embark, you make the voyage, you reach port, step ashore then. You'll be out of the grip of the pains and pleasures of this life, and thrall no longer to this earthen vessel." I'll never feel lonely, I conclude. What vexed me before? Oh yes: the mounds of dirt on fresh graves, how conspicuous they are as displacements of our loved ones below. What do they mean? What do they portend—those oval humps of black or red dirt molded as if by glaciers, mini-drumlins, like oversized armadillos playing possum, tucking their tails in so as not to give themselves away?

Winter Prayer

It's beginning to look a lot like November, I sing to myself crawling out of bed and looking out the window, sky as gray as a gray mule. It's been snowing since I woke. "No matter how far you drive you'll never reach the sun," Louis Jenkins writes in one of his poems, so I might as well forgive myself, I think, sitting on the toilet. Mid-morning, X and I hop in the car and drive toward Seneca Lake looking for something to do, drop in on a craft show in Hector, the crafters thankful for the blasting portable heaters, then pick up a few Honeycrisps at the Red Jacket fruit store in Geneva. The grand finale is in Watkins, at the south end of the lake: a tree decoration ceremony in their state park that skirts the edge of the lake, next to the Cargill plant, which is across the street from a little Italian bakery with the best cannoli in upstate New York. About a dozen others are at the park and the tree isn't any taller than I am and looks decorated already, rather sadly, we think. Not a whiff of a ceremony. Next to the tree is a small ice rink with one teenager looking tall in his skates and gliding across the surface. Then he stops and leans against the rail to chat up some girls watching. We stroll around and wind up in a newly built space the size of a basketball court, a tall ceiling, another young man there and he speaks to us, but the echo drowns him out and we laugh about it afterwards, how we asked him to repeat himself and still we couldn't fathom a word. It was like in a dream except no anxiety, not like the one I had after my father died: his back to me so I couldn't understand him and when he turned around I saw why—no mouth or jaw, or nose for that matter, just raw flesh where his face used to be. On the drive down, on the western side of the lake, the sun had broken through the clouds and had displayed some spectacular columns of light.

Something Strange

To consider myself dead: hard to do without consciousness riding piggy-back on the corpse. Maybe I'd want the sensations back: a spring storm rolling in and the smell of fresh cut grass, a herd of cattle on the hillside, Black Angus, or Holsteins with their patches of black and white, the taste of gin. Or I'd want the vision of the green terrain rolling like ocean waves. I catch myself wanting to be in those waves, willing to risk drowning just to feel the power of them lifting me up then dunking me deep. Philosophers say consciousness is consciousness *of* something. Make me feel something, we ask of a lover. Make me feel something celebratory and I'll do the same for you—we'll rise to celebrate not being unconscious. I've been keeping an eye on the changing moons these days, the mid-winter way their shapes depend on where they are in the sky, what time of night it is, or day. Some are small and straight up above and dim-looking through clouds, so I have to tilt my head all the way back; some on the horizon are clear and full like a bloated cow's belly; and some just a sliver or an orange quarter-moon at dusk halfway up its mountain of sky. I've been noting to myself that I don't understand the beauty of these figures and wish I did, but I'm also glad I don't. I want to watch them through the falling snow that catches light from streetlamps and not ask myself anything. I want to listen to the quiet crinkly sound sleet makes as it falls onto branches, or onto the already fallen snow on the ground.

Confrontation

There's nothing like walking in fresh snow, the joy of it, a childlike thing to relish. It can feel like floating right up to the sky and when you stop to rest it'll hold you in mid-air as if that blue sky-like substance were your mother or father. I saw out my window today footprints leading up to the porch and remembered smaller ones in another yard, another February under a different sky, two children playing in their winter gear, children with a mother, a father, a black lab. I watched the chair on my front porch rock back and forth in the wind, rocking and rocking. And there was a chair rocking in my head too and big flakes fell from everywhere like confetti. They were in it, old as they are, the children, waving goodbye in my head from atop a float crawling down the street, snow swirling about their heads. It all began as a love story rocking one child and then another in my arms and ended with me counting footprints in the snow as if they were years. The children counted the footprints leading out from the house, to an odd-shaped dwarf of a snowman. They counted—the older helping the younger—on and on like years the footprints, like blackbirds on powerlines. The footprints had little quarter-moon-shaped shadows in them dark as blackbirds. The children won't tell me why they're now quiet as footprints in snow. Everyone says it's just easier for them. When I now walk back across the yard from my mailbox or car, up to my shins or knees in the snow, making my way back to the porch, I try to step into my own footprints. It's just easier that way.

Ars Poetica

for Sandra Kohler

What is it that makes a poem sing, wail like a baby just pulled from some star in the night sky that had willed her into being? What if the poem is from a friend full of anger, an angry star shining, glimmering, whatever descriptor you like? Who looks at the night sky anymore, stars drowned out as they are? My friend writes a poem in which she fantasizes jumping off a balcony and into the audience below. She said it appeared slowly from her, a star coming out at dusk, her pain, her siblings' hatreds for one other, her parents' abuses and self-disdain, years of realizations in the making. Her poem crouches in a dark corner, a beauty nonetheless. I tell her so and she thanks me. I have been hurt, I think to myself. I have hurt others and have received the anger of those I've hurt. It is in that reception the poems lie, the jumping from the balcony, the being landed on. We're all being landed on, the bruises and scars sometimes not so conspicuous as to warn others, or ourselves, of what is always impending.

Dream

The other night I dreamed of a snake curled up in a mustard jar. I'm standing next to a wall in my living room and my wife hands me a jar of mustard with no lid on it, and when I look down the mustard in the jar has turned into a snake, a mustard-colored snake, which is logical within the logic of the dream, I suppose. I suppose too there's something Edenic about this dream—man, woman, snake—but I'm not pursuing that line of thought and, besides, I doubt there were mustard jars in the Garden of Eden. Then again, mustard is a common Middle Eastern garden plant and field crop and there's a parable about it in Matthew. So to keep the snake from crawling out of the jar I place the top of it, the open end of it, against the living room wall like I'm trapping a bug, but the snake miraculously slides right into the wall. I wondered what it was about, the dream. Maybe I'm yearning for my "Garden of Eden" because that's where I was not so laden with grown-up thoughts—desires, ambitions, guilt. Innocence is what gets sloughed off as you grow into adulthood, like a snake its skin. Once we begin our adult relationships and the pursuit of those oh-so-interesting desires with a desperation we think is warranted by their intensity, who of those that stand in our way can dodge our bullets—bullets aimed at our loved ones? And what chance have we to dodge the bullets of those who love us, or that special someone we love, or once loved?

In another dream, this one from last night, I'm at a family reunion with my older sister who died in a nursing home in Oklahoma City eleven years ago this month, maybe even this week, maybe even today or yesterday, the day of the night of this dream. In the dream, my sister won't hug me straight on—she keeps walking up to me and turning to stand beside me. She was ten years older and a surrogate mother to me, since our mother, as much as she loved us, was far too busy taking care of all five of us children—cooking, cleaning, working her job—to dote on each of us. So my sister took up the slack and was dear to me, thus her unexpected death at sixty-five being such a blow. In the dream she is standing next to me and not facing me, avoiding eye contact, which is disconcerting because, I realize as I'm writing this, in the dream I am yearning for it. I also do not realize in the dream that in reality she is dead, which means she's dead in the dream, which is disconcerting as well. If I had known, maybe I could've confessed to her how sorry I am that she had such a difficult life and death. I wonder how consoling to me it might've been. You see, a few years ago I published an essay about her death, a gruesome few days for her and I describe it graphically. The dream may be a reflection of my suspicion that the essay violated a sense of propriety, as well as a sense of trust she may have had in me. She was not herself those last few days, paranoid and confused. At one point she asked if she had ever married or had had children. It was a brutal death. My thirty-something son found the essay offensive. He's not speaking to me these days. I left his mother when she was pregnant with him and now in his middle age he has rejected me.

In the dream the other family members standing around at this reunion—aunts, uncles, cousins—begin urging me to attend to a TV behind me that has fallen onto the floor. The TV is similar to a Sony model my son's mother and I bought in 1982, except it has a hole in the screen so big you can see daylight through it. Then I'm holding the TV in my arms like how you'd hold a baby even though in reality the TV was too heavy for that, but I suppose that's the nature of dreams, where the mind has messages it considers so importantly insightful that when it's attempting to jolt us out of our amnesia, if it were to adhere to the laws of nature it would fail—everyday imagery would muddle its message and leave the insight suppressed. It must employ outrageous surrealism to point us in the direction of what it thinks we need to know. Freud said something similar about the function of uncanny experiences, that they are our mind's attempts to recover suppressed memories or understandings too disruptive or painful to bear, what we've had to estrange ourselves from to make our lives livable. In the dream, I'm holding the TV and looking over my shoulder at my aunts, uncles, and cousins who are still yelling at me to notice the hole in it. It's as if a Velociraptor were about to eat me and my relatives are warning me of my impending slaughter. The hole in the TV might represent a gap in my life associated with it—my son, of course. Perhaps I feel my lapsed family connections are threatening to devour me, or worse, pull me down into nothingness.

Winter Stroll

My wife and I take a walk through the streets of our neighborhood this afternoon, late winter, fat snowflakes swirling all around us like confetti, or like flocks of migrating monarch butterflies except they're snow-white and migrating into our neighborhood. It seems as if time itself is falling from the sky and coming down around us in bits and pieces. My life becomes the walk and the walk takes on the length of my life. A car passes and it's a year of my youth driving away, a man in a cap at the steering wheel who could be me on his way home or to the store, but I think it's my father and I wonder where he's going, having been buried in the red dirt of Oklahoma the past twenty years. Then a black lab walks by ahead of its owner and I notice a snowflake on the tip of its nose that becomes the weeks I spent in a hospital as a young man recovering from a car accident. I was released from the hospital with a few scars across my belly but alive, breathing, eating, pissing, and shitting like a normal person, not someone who'd vanished like a snowflake on a dog's nose. Then we pass a house and it becomes the house I was born into, with split-level stairs I remember often tripping down, and there in the house is a bookcase with rows of different-colored books. Then we come across some puddles with snowflakes falling into them and melting to become a part of them, and one of the puddles becomes the town swimming pool I learned to swim in as a boy during hot Oklahoma summers. I remember diving from the boards and climbing out of the water and up a ladder, my skin smelling like chlorine, and running to the concession stand to buy a popsicle or one of those grape or cherry lollipops for a quarter that would win you another one just like it if it had a "winner" sticker on it, which was rarely the case. And rarely the case becomes how often I was to win in love as a teenager, the love lasting only as long as it took to lick that lollipop down to nothing, but when I look up and across the street I see myself just a few months older sitting on a picnic table in the park with my first girlfriend, whose heart I would break a few weeks later. We're kissing as if we would never have another lover. Then my wife and I come to the orchard on Seneca Street and the apple tree on the corner becomes the mimosa tree in the front yard of the house I grew up in, a tree I climbed into so often its limbs became like my mother's arms. I remember springtime every year its white blossoms would fall around our heads, swirling as if they too were pieces of time, as if everyone in the neighborhood was living in their own universe of experiences, seconds, days, weeks, months, years of memories swirling around them, like these large snowflakes falling on the bare limbs of the apple trees.

Reality

Some say it is what it is, a tautology, but go stand hatless in a downpour you'll see what that means. Or neck-up in a swimming pool under a sky lit up by lightning. Then again, some say it is what you see it as, and we know that to be true as well—stand up to a bully and the sun will shine on your head differently, more warmly, brighter. Then some say it is what you make of it—a cancer patient may say his illness is a blessing, inviting an expansion of consciousness. Then there's the phrase "It's the story I tell myself," displaying a double-layered perception: truth here, story there. What is it really? All those and more, of course. A doctor once had to reopen a hole in my abdomen to insert a tube there and didn't think it needed numbing. Came to my bedside like a priest, a shaman with a sacred headband, weed, and pipe, and laid out a set of pencil-length steel tools, each with a ball on the end a little larger than the next, except the first one, of course, and when he started in with them the moment became what it was, what I was perceiving it as, and what I wanted to make of it.

Love Poem

In the hospital as a young man—car accident, three months in ICU, four abdominal operations—I fall in love with her. Every four hours into my thigh or butt, toward the end of which, around hour three, I watch the door and listen and listen for footsteps, the syringe in the white uniform, beautiful hair and eyes, who would call me by my name and ask me to roll over or lift up my gown to show my thigh. That syringe's name was Anna, Marlene, Joan, had a New Orleans or Tennessee accent and the point at which her point would meet its subcutaneous hotspot was where my belief in god would become my belief in her, a flavor, a taste on my tongue, a love in my marrow for all living things.

To Live

It's April again and winter hangs on by a spider's thread, crocuses flashing their yellows and purples, weeping willows with their wispy costumes looking like ghosts from afar, Japanese magnolias dropping their blossoms already, bushes everywhere threatening to push out buds like those tiny fingers we see in pictures of embryos. Even irises are up, their shoots pointing at the sky in astonishment. Look! It's almost here! Certainly no one wants to shovel snow; no one wants to heave onto their backs once again the winter gear. We want to see dark clouds pregnant with rain rolling into the neighborhood with lightning on their tails. We want thunderheads to shoot up like the skyscrapers we know them to be. How many more springs will I be rewarded? That's what we are, are we not? Seasons one after the other? We want to see ourselves in another and another like fresh-breasted robins hopping from worm to worm wriggling out of the soil. That's us too, wriggling out of the soil. Raw desire. We want to see forsythia showing off their "bloomers" (saucy forsythia!). We want to see young cosmos swaying in the warm, pre-storm wind like flamenco dancers twisting their torsos, chins up high, arms swaying. We want to see rain pour down like music to make the flowers dance in the wind. Would I come back, I ask myself, as an early cosmos swaying in the breeze? What about a trillium or snowdrop or spring beauty or johnny jump up? A squirrel or bluejay or snowy owl swooping down on a field mouse? What about a field mouse? Would I come back as a field mouse swooped down upon by a snowy owl? Yes! Yes I would! Name it and I will live it! A tree even. What about tree bark or a leaf or a mite on a leaf? A caterpillar munching on it? A microbe in a drop of rainwater on the leaf, or on a fresh blade of grass? What about a flea? Would I be a flea in an alley cat's fur? What about flea poop? Would I come back as flea poop? Tiny spots of half-digested blood on a dog's belly or a possum's crotch? Yes. Yes, I would.

On the Easing of Tensions

We're told Gautama achieved his first yogic state when he was a boy after witnessing the carnage of a plowed field. He felt intense sorrow for the lives he saw destroyed—insects, young grasses, other plants—and then an ensuing joy in recognition of his own being. He sat in the shade of a rose-apple tree in the asana position, straight back, crossed legs, and it was said the shade stayed with him the whole day, a miracle. He remembered this state of ecstasy years later when he was near death from his yogic fasting, and the memory made him realize he needn't fight his body to achieve a joyful release. Karen Armstrong tells us the prime insight of the axial age is that the sacred is an inherent aspect of the self and yet, she wrote, practitioners—yogis & other Hindus—found the eternal self difficult to access. The premise here regarding my own sorrows is the recent shootings we in this country are unable to avoid. A new one just yesterday, children in a small Texas town. How deep the rage for someone to take it out on children. I don't know if I find the sacred difficult to access, but with these tragedies I'm not sure what or where it is. We have the word agnostic, connoting an ambivalence regarding a belief in the sacred or a higher being, but some agnostics are more proactive. Agnostic theists, for example, hold that the sacred cannot be known. I ask, can it not be known and nonetheless felt in the body, which can be a fickle instrument, as we know—you're hungover or in a foul mood because of a recent injury, a strained ligament in your shoulder or knee and it's throbbing, or you've had a tiff with your spouse and want your life to be free of such vexations. You feel them in your body and can't help projecting them onto the world. So much depends on what you deem important. I was walking a trail yesterday in a state park, a beautiful spring morning, and the couple ahead of me was walking a dog who kept looking back at me, a yellow- and black-spotted boxer. The couple seemed in the midst of an intense exchange, but the dog seemed more interested in me, the look on his face when he turned around sad and solicitous, a reflection of its grief perhaps. If that perception is accurate, then I say the feeling was mutual and I stopped to give us all some distance.

The Terror of History

I remember as a boy in early or mid-spring watching hordes of June bugs spread themselves out under the streetlights at night. This was in the small town I grew up in in western Oklahoma called Clinton, named after Judge Clinton Irwin, an Illinois lawyer of Irish descent. The town was bought in 1899 by two white men from four Indians: Hays, Shoe-Boy, Nowahy, and Night Killer. My family's house was in a little development on the western edge of town, across the street from a nursing home and funeral parlor. I would sit under the streetlights after the sun had gone down and watch the bugs squirm, hundreds, maybe thousands, and wonder who they were. Maybe they were ghosts watching us under the light, watching me on the curb. Maybe they were my grandparents and their dead parents and grandparents, some of whom had tried to farm the dry land in Washita County a few miles west of town and had failed. Maybe one was my great grandmother who tripped over a wagon tongue pregnant with her seventh and bled to death before my great grandfather could find a doctor, leaving my 16-year-old grandmother, the oldest, to mother the others. She went on to birth ten of her own and I came to know her. Maybe they were the ghosts of those who'd been there for hundreds of years, descendants of those who'd migrated from Beringia, themselves descendants of northern Siberians who'd migrated in the centuries before. Some Beringians went east along the Arctic circle and settled as far as Greenland, some went south and somewhere near what is now Montana split again, some going farther south and some east to where I live in upstate New York.

In early spring, when the snow geese have arrived here, in a marsh called Muck Flats, where routes 89 and 31 meet, my wife and I like to go watch them chat with one another while grazing. A stunning scene, 3 to 400,000. This is north of Montezuma National Wildlife Refuge on Cayuga Lake. Cayuga, "The People of the Great Swamp," of the Haudenosaunee Nations, "people of the longhouses," whose social structure was matrilineal, such that the women lived in single longhouses with their husbands (of their own matrilineages) in villages of a few longhouses to as many as fifty. In 1778, George Washington ordered them driven out or slaughtered because they had sided with the British and were still fighting alongside them with the loyalist Colonel John Butler, killing patriots and raiding European settlements in New York and Pennsylvania and taking prisoners. These raids forced settlements to be abandoned, settlements encroaching on land promised the Haudenosaunee by the British in 1701, in the Treaty of Albany, and later that same year by the French as well. So from June to October, 1779, 6200 troops, led by generals John Sullivan and James Clinton, destroyed over forty Indigenous settlements—Cayuga, Seneca, Onondaga—burning crops and orchards all the way to the British fort of

Niagara, where thousands of Haudenosaunee spent that winter starving, in spite of attempts by the British to supply them. Some escaped and dispersed to Canada or Ohio and some were later moved to a territory called Oklahoma. There are monuments around here commemorating generals Sullivan and Clinton, one close by outside of the small village of Ovid, which overlooks beautiful Seneca Lake, a forty-mile body of water that's deepest of all the Finger Lakes, over 700 feet deep. Not nearly as deep as its natural history, with its glaciers that melted ten thousand years ago and its ocean floors that spread themselves out here millions of years earlier.

Vox Nihili

It's June and the early evening light makes its way through the red bud tree, spilling its puddles of light onto grass. Someone in the distance is mowing their lawn, the buzzing reminding me there will be a time when I'll no longer hear it, the sound of consciousness. When the buzzing stops, I'll note to myself how lovely the silence is. Will there be that recognition in the hereafter? "How lovely it was," I will remark to the soul next to me, "but how lovelier it is now in the quiet night. By the way, where are we and why wasn't I told of this place, I mean in a way that would make me believe it? Not by the fairytale wings-of-an-angel method only children can be expected to believe, but in a grownup broccoli-and-carrot-soup sort of way." "Listen," the soul will say. "This is the truth of it: there's nothing grand here—this is you after you've breathed your last breath, said your last goodbyes, people you knew and loved still crying, if you're lucky, that is. Look at them," the soul will continue, "the ones who knew you, appreciated your virtues, forgiven you your faults. Just lay your head down and sing along with the rest of us because we don't exist anymore. We don't exist any more than did those angel's wings in your dreams when you were alive and breathed the air you used to breathe and drank that sweet water you'll never drink again. Listen to the silence in your head and bask in it. Trust that it's lovelier than your mother's voice singing you to sleep, lovelier than the sound of waterfalls, tree frogs, and cicadas, lovelier than the sound of faraway thunder."

The Verbalist

Language is life, creating its own value, a jellyfish floating just beneath the water's surface that defies a shape other than what you see it as, a half-deflated balloon, a flamenco dress, a breathing lampshade, a vagina swimming in the sea. When I was a boy the most popular game we played was army. In the cool morning or sweltering afternoon, we'd find long sticks for rifles and shorter ones for "potato mashers," those Nazi hand grenades named after the kitchen instrument, implying a certain un-finessed quality, a bluntness of purpose (Coleridge said metaphors never walk on all fours). We'd run around the neighborhood making gun noises and hide behind corners in bushes, or high in trees hoping one of our unobservant friends would walk past and then we'd have a decision on our hands: fall down on them, risking pain and injury, or blast them with sounds and hope they'd take their death "like a man." The drop-down is what you'd choose, of course, which would leave you groaning and checking your arms and legs where bruises would likely appear the next day, before both of you would break out laughing. This is not real war, of course—this is the verbalist who doesn't use rhetoric or earnest intention because he's just talking for talking's sake, presumably, that is—unless he doesn't know what he's saying is just air in a balloon that nobody wants to hear. Sometimes we must confess we don't know when we're doing it, and even then that balloon racing across the room can startle you into recognizing a truth you couldn't have known. Maybe the air is consoling a friend who's down on herself by fleshing out a generous argument you think is going nowhere. The words confess feelings for your friend that makes her feel better because she knows you have no ulterior motive, ostensibly, that is, because jellyfish can take the shape of a new species, a new dance, a new flamenco of meaning, the dress swirling and swirling until you're giddy with insights into your own intentions, ulterior motives your verbiage gives shape to. That play army scene, for example, points to the fact that men will drum up, rationalize, find false warrants for, pretexts, for an activity so closely resembling what they played as children we might suspect that as children they were not mimicking war at all, but creating a warrant for when as warriors they would reenact the love for one another they felt as boys. Verbiage can do that, make truth come out *come out wherever you are!* like a child hiding under a staircase waiting to be found.

Imagining

What would it be like?...another reality. Would it be without tires, without KFC, our toes with no nails? Maybe leaves would turn blue in the fall, grow out black in the spring. Dogs meow, kittens bark. Would plants walk and cattle plant themselves in the soil, their necks as long as giraffes' necks or like vines reaching up for the sun? Would there even be books? Maybe books would be creatures crawling out of the ocean like those early fish with legs. Maybe they'd eat and sleep and shit like the rest of us. Books that would shit in our yards and look at us with guilty expressions and we'd be compelled to clean up after them. Maybe there'd be no language at all, except what drips from the sky or bubbles up thick from the ground like oil. Strange sounds falling down or rising up into our unsuspecting ears, sounds like *multi-bubbliciocity* and *octo-generocantorousness*. Maybe flying fish would build their nests in trees. And what would be the cost of things? Would we trade bundles of hair for food, maybe open our mouths and let the air nourish us, leave us sated and scratching our fat bellies? Would there be feelings we've never had? Would love be hatred or indifference? Might ire be satisfaction, happiness melancholy? Would parents trade their babies, swap them around? Maybe babies would rule the earth, newborns born wise knowing who to trust, who to banish, who to listen to for laws, what leaders to insist be sent back to school. Maybe we would all grow up as something else, crocodiles, tarantulas, doves, sea turtles, perch. Maybe the sky would be our temple, the fishes our gods and goddesses.

On Time

My father used to say if you're not early you're late. A typical time-is-money idea, though maybe it has more to do with showing people respect. Don't waste people's time with your thoughtlessness. But if it's true that if you're not early you're late, then there's no such thing as *on time*. Time becomes a true mystery and in some respects doesn't exist at all. It's certainly not *now* because now is always already gone, which means it never was. So what is it? Maybe a thing, a what or a who? Maybe it's everything, or whatever we want it to be. Maybe it's a dog, or a flea—if so, what sex? Do fleas have sex? Of course they do but who wears the pants in those relationships, and are they relationships? Does time wear pants? Small and tight, or loose like dancer pants? Maybe time is music? Musicians swear by it, as it determines meaning: cheerful, quick, jaunty, like at a wedding; bellicose, loud, angry, a battle march; sad, somber, and slow, a dirge. Maybe time is dance, offering music a visible form like what leaves offer breezes. Here breeze, the leaves say, let me be your costume, your pants, your apron, your skirt and blouse—whatever you wish. But if time is a dance, which one? a samba? a flamenco? a tango? a Texas two-step?

Wait, does time have legs? Oh yes—travels well and can shuffle to beat the band, can run like a hurricane and, as we all know, it can fly. Can slow down to the limit when attended to, but sometimes it speeds like a demon. Time *is* a demon. But it doesn't fear the flashing lights in the rear-view mirror, because it also is a rear-view mirror, for me sometimes nothing but, blocking my view of the road, blinding even. I'm shocked by how ugly it is what I've seen there. Lies, betrayals, thoughtlessness. What was I thinking? Does time think? Maybe it's a Zen master playing-it-as-it-goes. Or a BIG THINKER—a monist, a nominalist, a non-compatibilist, a Manichean, a dualist, or maybe an antinomian. Antinomians reject Mosaic Law and hold that faith alone confers on us God's blessing. As in *Genesis*, when God asks Abraham to trust him and promises nothing but as many progeny as there are stars in the night sky. A beautiful promise, I suppose, as many children as there are stars in the night sky, though not for me, thank you.

Was any part of God's promise, I wonder, a promise of beauty itself? Is time beautiful? A heart-shaped face, full lips, cheeks flushed. Perhaps a masculine beauty, a jawline to die for, Paul Newman eyes. The philosopher Henri Bergson said time keeps everything from happening at once. I suppose as such it secures our welfare, keeps us from blinding one another with...what? Why, eternity of course! Maybe Bergson means it can't be stripped bare of its existential qualities, its haecceity, as Duns Scotus called it, Heidegger's Dasein—what makes everything so *real?* Some say time is a river—does that mean it flows out of our frame of reference, beyond our horizon, past our understanding? I'm afraid time exists only in the moment, essence-less. So yes, it is a river, but that ain't no metaphor, for time *is* the river. It is the river and the sky and the drifting clouds and a scampering squirrel and a blade of grass blowing in the breeze. It's a crawdad under a rock, an ant on your leg, your bladder pressuring you to go, your morning hunger for breakfast and a decent cup of coffee.

On a branch
Floating down the river
A cricket, singing
Issa

What to make of *deep* time? Dinosaurs dominating the ecosystem for 185 million years, give or take a few mill, and even that's a mere teardrop in the stretch of it all! Can we fathom that? Must time always be, for us, concrete? a mere image? Dangling legs on an air-born wasp? An ancient tree, a redwood, a scarred tree bark, shagbark hickory with its deep ravines running up and down itself. Or smooth like white birch bark, what Indigenous peoples of North America, it is said, used to write on and perhaps still do. "It is written," Christians and Muslims proclaim, but pray tell what *on*? papyrus? shale? beach sand? whale skin? oyster shell? the skin on your back? the back of your hand? Is time the skin on the back of your hand?

Oh, the stories we tell one another, betrayals, murders, deceits, sibling rivalries, parents favoring one child over another or abandoning them altogether. Kindnesses too, I suppose, forgivenesses, redemptions, promises of love and loyalty, vows of young lovers and their devotion, loving voices to one another, promising children, well nurtured, tenderly loved. Of course, time can be all of that. As calm as a mother singing her baby to sleep, a lullaby of lilting sounds, voices, the stories lulling the baby down to a long rest as it lays all its trials and tribulations at time's feet. It never ends, time, endless as a bottomless sky, a gentle blue, at times a dark whirling dervish from above, or from the sea, waves forcing themselves onto land, tsunami surprises. But time can be simple as well, as simple as a meal, for life isn't much more than that, a meal to relish, to savor, to imbibe, to appreciate and drink in, to sate our unquenchable hungers and thirsts, needs and desires, yearnings stretching out over hours and hours turning into days and weeks and years—rich and complex, unfathomable flavors and, afterwards, long peaceful nights to dream our dreams by.

www.ingramcontent.com/pod-product-compliance
Lightning Source LLC
LaVergne TN
LVHW090539110826

845146LV00003B/1177

* 9 7 9 8 8 9 9 9 0 4 6 7 7 *